I can make a
Word

Written by Viv Lambert, illustrated by Rowan Clifford

How to use this book…

1) Look at the picture, say the name of each labelled object

2) Find the stickers, using the picture to help

3) Read all the words, identifying the sounds of the missing letters

4) Write the words in the spaces

Find the missing letters to complete the picture and the words. What do the words say?

Write these words.

Find the picture sticker which starts with each of the letter sounds. Then write the first letter of each word.

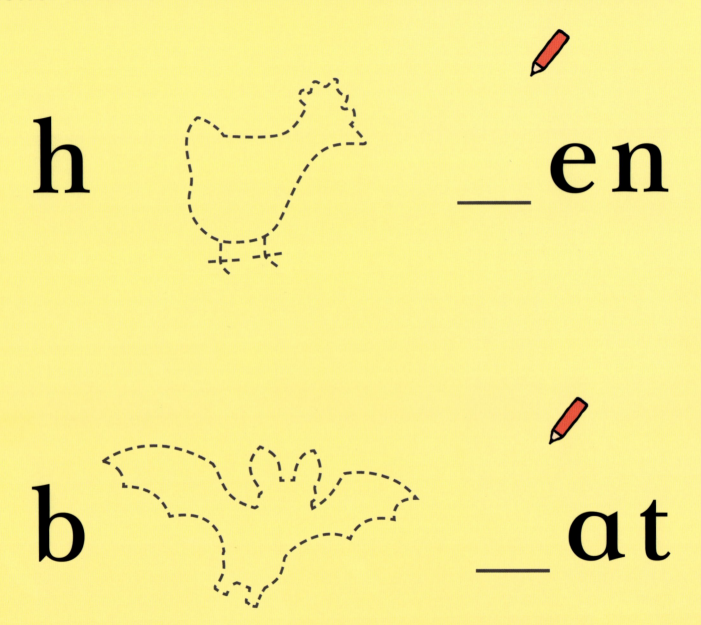

p _ig

f _ox

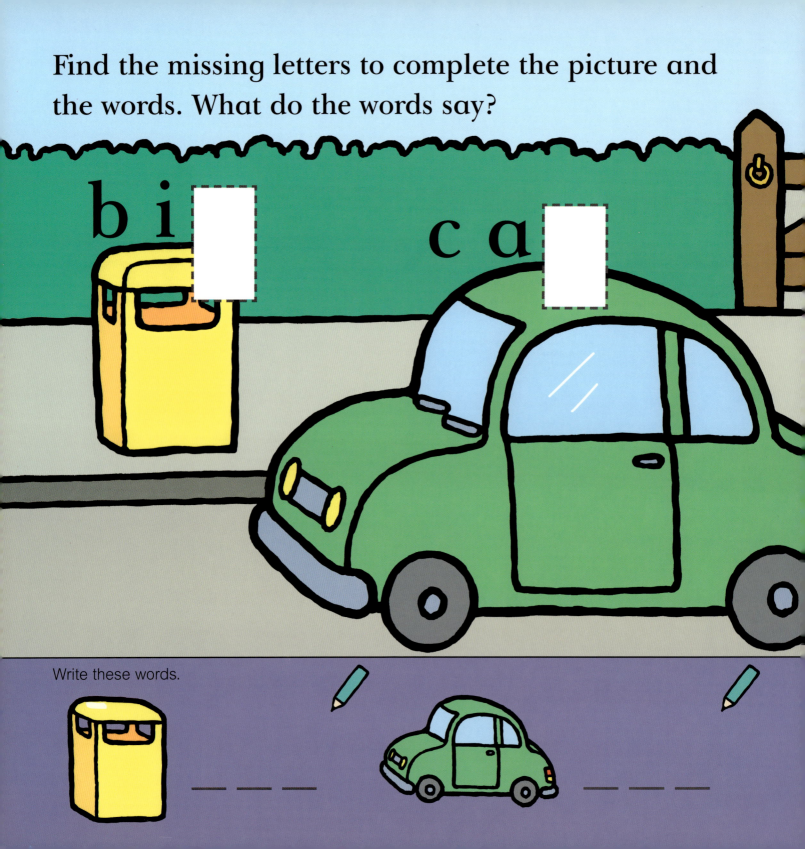

Find the sticker which completes each word and shows what it says. Then write the last letter of each word.

pa   pa_

ba   ba_

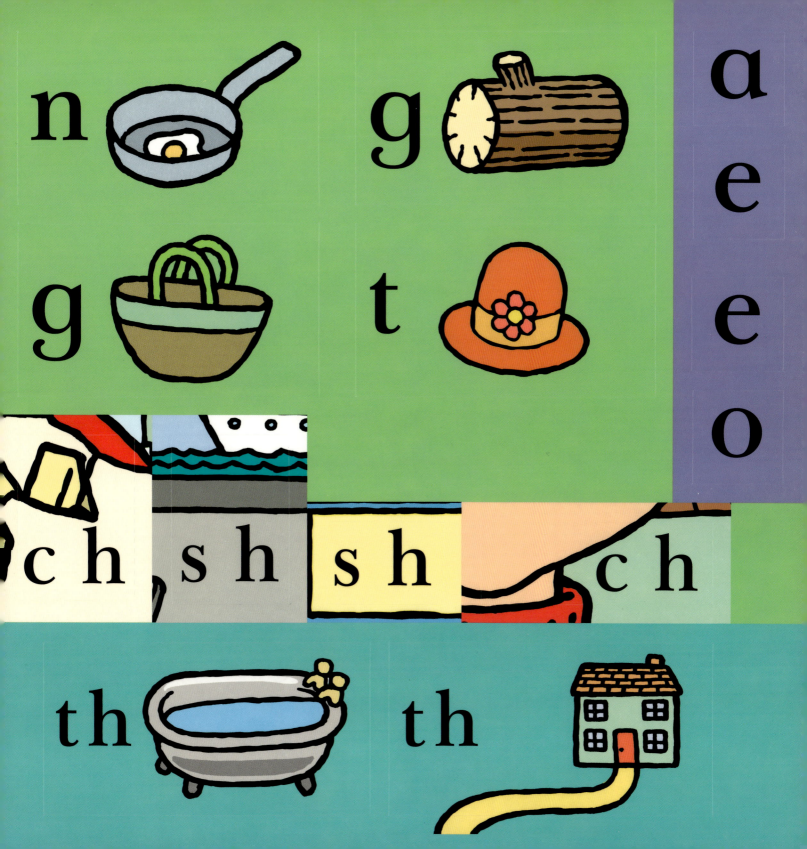

lo   lo_

ha   ha_

Find the missing letters to complete the picture and the words. What do the words say?

Write these words.

Finish these words by putting the right letter sticker in the middle. Then write the middle letter of each word.

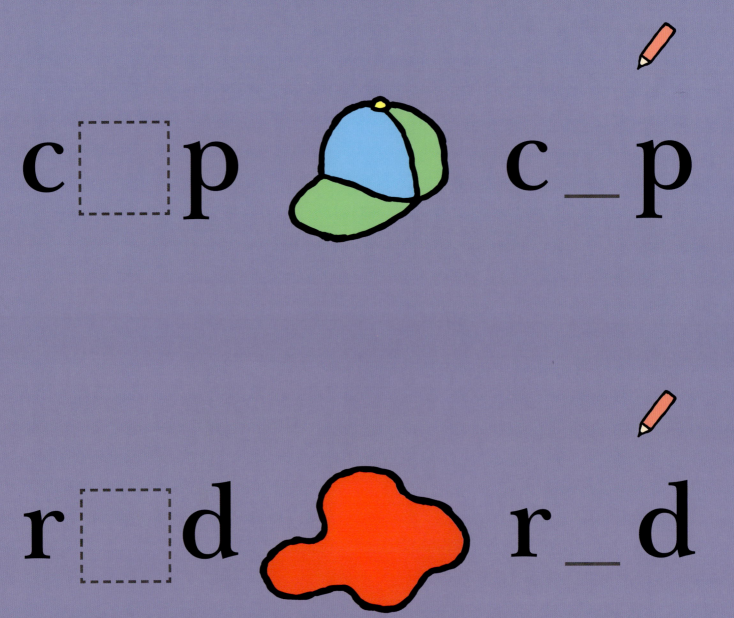

p [ ] t      p _ t

b [ ] x      b _ x

Find the sticker which completes each word and shows what it says. Then write the words again in the spaces.

ba _ _ _ _ _

pa _ _ _ _ _